Made in the USA
Columbia, SC
21 July 2021

42203924R00067